Richard M. Nixon

The Presidents of the United States

George Washington
1789–1797

John Adams
1797–1801

Thomas Jefferson
1801–1809

James Madison
1809–1817

James Monroe
1817–1825

John Quincy Adams
1825–1829

Andrew Jackson
1829–1837

Martin Van Buren
1837–1841

William Henry Harrison
1841

John Tyler
1841–1845

James Polk
1845–1849

Zachary Taylor
1849–1850

Millard Fillmore
1850–1853

Franklin Pierce
1853–1857

James Buchanan
1857–1861

Abraham Lincoln
1861–1865

Andrew Johnson
1865–1869

Ulysses S. Grant
1869–1877

Rutherford B. Hayes
1877–1881

James Garfield
1881

Chester Arthur
1881–1885

Grover Cleveland
1885–1889

Benjamin Harrison
1889–1893

Grover Cleveland
1893–1897

William McKinley
1897–1901

Theodore Roosevelt
1901–1909

William H. Taft
1909–1913

Woodrow Wilson
1913–1921

Warren Harding
1921–1923

Calvin Coolidge
1923–1929

Herbert Hoover
1929–1933

Franklin D. Roosevelt
1933–1945

Harry Truman
1945–1953

Dwight Eisenhower
1953–1961

John F. Kennedy
1961–1963

Lyndon Johnson
1963–1969

Richard Nixon
1969–1974

Gerald Ford
1974–1977

Jimmy Carter
1977–1981

Ronald Reagan
1981–1989

George H. W. Bush
1989–1993

William J. Clinton
1993–2001

George W. Bush
2001–present

RICHARD M. NIXON

BILLY ARONSON

Marshall Cavendish
Benchmark
New York

Marshall Cavendish Benchmark
99 White Plains Road
Tarrytown, NY 10591-9001
www.marshallcavendish.us

Copyright © 2008 by Billy Aronson
All rights reserved.
No part of this book may be reproduced in any form without the written permission of the publisher.

All Internet sites were correct and accurate at time of printing.

Library of Congress Cataloging-in-Publication Data

Aronson, Billy.
Richard M. Nixon/by Billy Aronson
p. cm.—(Presidents and their times)
Summary: "This series provides comprehensive information on the presidents of the United States and places each within his historical and cultural context. It also explores the formative events of his times and how he responds"—Provided by publisher.
Includes bibliographical references and index.
ISBN 978-0-7614-2428-4
1. Nixon, Richard M. (Richard Milhous), 1913–1994—Juvenile literature. 2 Presidents—United States—Biography—Juvenile literature. 3. United States—Politics and government—1969–1974—Juvenile literature. I. Title. II. Series.
E856.A893 2007
973.924092—dc22 2006013839

Editor: Christine Florie
Publisher: Michelle Bisson
Editorial Director: Michelle Bisson
Art Director: Anahid Hamparian
Series Designer: Alex Ferrari

Photo research by Connie Gardner

Cover Photo by The Granger Collection

The photographs in this book are used by permission and courtesy of: *The Granger Collection:* 6, 87 (L); *Corbis:* 28, 30,49, 78; Wally McNamee, 4, 40, 79, 85, 87 (R); Lee Stone/Sygma, 80; Lee Snider, 67; Bettmann, 8, 12, 14, 17, 18, 19, 21, 26, 29, 35, 39, 42, 45, 50, 58, 59, 63, 65, 71, 76, 86 (L); Ted Streshinsky, 51; JP Laffont/Sygma, 57; *The Image Works:* Topham, 9, 86 (R); *Getty Images:* Hulton Archive, 10, 15, 72; AFP/AFP, 23; Time Life Pictures, 24, 27, 43, 56, 69; *AP Photo:* 32, 47, 53, 68; *Magnum Photos:* Philip Jones Griffiths, 36.

Printed in Malaysia
1 3 5 6 4 2

CONTENTS

"You've got to learn to survive defeat. That's when you develop character."

—Richard M. Nixon

THE YOUNG NIXON

*T*he amount of information available about Richard Nixon is overwhelming. Besides the countless books, articles, and essays written about him, Nixon himself has written ten books, including a memoir of more than a thousand pages. He also has left behind taped recordings containing over four thousand hours of his private conversations.

Despite all this information, many presidential experts claim that they still do not know who Richard Nixon really was. They are confused about the true nature of his character and uncertain about his genuine beliefs. Historian Theodore H. White admits, "I have spent the greatest portion of my adult life writing about Richard Nixon and I still don't understand him."

Many of Nixon's closest associates share this confusion. His former chief of staff, H. R. "Bob" Haldeman, remembers Nixon as "the strangest man I ever met." Historian Garry Wills once suggested that Nixon was impossible to know because there was nothing real about him. "He is the least authentic man alive," Wills claimed.

The difficulty in pinning down Nixon's character has not prevented Americans from having strong feelings about him. Throughout his career, Nixon had followers who loved him and critics who despised him. Supporters would describe a hardworking patriot who was elected vice president twice and president twice. In their eyes, he led America through a turbulent period, brought an end to a long war, and opened the door to lasting peace. Enemies would describe a chronic liar who won elections by ruining his opponents' reputations and selecting issues only to win votes. They saw a man who rose to fame by stirring fear and using dirty tricks to keep his power, until he was finally caught and became the first president forced to resign.

Although there is disagreement about who Nixon was, there is no debate that he had an enormous impact on his nation and on the world. At Nixon's funeral, Senator Robert Dole proclaimed that the second half of the twentieth century was the Age of Nixon.

Nixon at age three and a half (far right), with his parents Frank and Hannah, brothers Harold (left), and Donald.

CHILDHOOD

Nixon's controversial and complex life began in a simple place: a small town in the California desert called Yorba Linda. He was born on January 19, 1913. Nixon's parents, Frank and Hannah, named him Richard after the English king Richard the Lionhearted. His middle name, Milhous, was his mother's maiden name. At the time of Richard's birth, the couple already had a son named Harold. Over the coming years, three more boys, Donald, Arthur, and Edward, joined the family.

Hannah Nixon was a strict Quaker who had grown up speaking plain speech, a traditional type of speech that uses formal words like thee and thou. Frank was Methodist but became a Quaker after marrying Hannah. Deeply committed to their faith, Frank and Hannah took the boys to church every Wednesday evening and several times each Sunday.

Nixon was a bright boy who learned to read before he was five.

Although members of the Nixon family prayed and played together, they rarely expressed their love for one another openly. Richard never saw his parents hug or kiss one another, and he never once heard his mother say she loved him. There were open expressions of anger, however, particularly by Richard's father. Frank was a strict disciplinarian who would punish the boys by striking them with a ruler or a belt.

At a young age, Richard became known as the quiet and smart boy in the family. Hannah taught him to read the newspaper and to play the piano before he was five years old. Besides enjoying reading and music, Richard was fascinated by trains. "Sometimes at night," he would later write, "I was awakened by the whistle stop of a train, and then I dreamed of the far-off places I wanted to visit someday."

When Richard was nine, his father's business was failing. Frank was a lemon farmer, and business was so bad that at times the family had only cornmeal to eat. In 1922 Frank gave up trying to earn a living with the lemon grove. He moved the family to the nearby town of Whittier, where he opened a grocery store. The whole family helped out in the store. And over the years Richard took additional jobs to help out with expenses. He worked as a chicken plucker, a janitor at a swimming pool, and a barker at an amusement park.

The Nixons found a way to win their battle against poverty, but they soon faced an obstacle they could not defeat. Richard's

Young Richard Nixon (top left) with brothers Harold, Arthur, and Donald (in tire).

Nixon Family Values

Richard Nixon's career would take him far from Yorba Linda, but the lessons he received from his parents would stay with him always. Nixon remembered his father as a gifted speaker who loved to argue. Frank taught Richard key lessons about debating that would help him in politics.

In one of Richard's first high-school debates, he was assigned to prove that insects do more good than harm. Considering insects to be disgusting creatures, Richard felt sure he would lose the debate. Richard's father took him to a butterfly expert who explained that without bees to carry pollen, many leafy plants would die. Frank urged him to stick with this one argument, and Richard went on to win the debate. Over the course of his career, Nixon would win debates, lawsuits, and elections by making one strong, simple point and hammering it home.

"My mother was a saint," Nixon said in his last speech before leaving the White House. Throughout his life Nixon would praise the selfless sacrifices his mother made, particularly as she cared for her dying sons. He would also speak of the generosity she had shown needy people who came to the family store. Hannah tried to pass on to her son her basic values and the faith from which she derived them. As Richard became caught up in politics, his mother grew concerned. On the day of his inauguration as vice president, she gave him a note that said,

You have gone far and we are proud of you always. I know that you will keep your relationship with your maker as it should be for after all that, as you must know, is the most important thing in this life.

Richard put the note in his wallet and kept it with him for the rest of his life.

youngest brother, Arthur, contracted a lung disease called tuber-culosis, which was then considered incurable. He died at the age of seven. While Arthur's struggle was brief, Richard's older brother, Harold, endured the disease for years before it finally took his life. Hannah believed that the deaths of Richard's brothers inspired him to work harder to make his parents proud.

COLLEGE DAYS

When it was time for college, Nixon's excellent grades won him a scholarship to Yale University in Connecticut. Nixon could not afford the cost of living away from home, so he enrolled at Whittier College.

Nixon (number 23, above) said of his college football career, "I got into a few games after they were hopelessly won or hopelessly lost, . . . when they put the substitutes in, and finally the water boy, and then me."

Nixon had a busy extra-curricular life at Whittier. He joined the debate team and served as president of the student body. He also acted in plays. His sloping nose and puffy cheeks made him perfect for quirky character roles.

Playing on the football team had a lasting effect on Nixon. He was the team's weakest player, but his coach, Wallace "Chief" Newman, inspired Nixon to endure pain and to fight like he had never fought before. "There is no way I can adequately describe Chief Newman's influence on me," Richard would one day write. "He drilled into me a competitive spirit and the determination to come back after you have been knocked down or after you lose."

After graduating second in his class from Whittier, Nixon went on to Duke University Law School in North Carolina. Even though he had a scholarship to pay for his education, he had to work in the library to pay for living expenses. At one point during these years, Nixon was so poor that he had to live in a shack with no heat or indoor plumbing. In spite of such discomforts, he was able to study hard, eventually graduating third in his class.

After receiving his law degree, Nixon took a job at a law firm in Whittier and devoted his free time to acting at a local community theater. At auditions for one production, he met a tall schoolteacher named Thelma Catherine "Pat" Ryan whose lively personality and red hair captivated him. When Nixon asked Ryan for a date, she told him that she was too busy. He replied, "You shouldn't say that, because someday I'm going to marry you."

In the days following this bold prediction, Nixon kept pestering Ryan for a date, and she kept refusing. He even began chauffeuring her on her dates, simply to stay in her thoughts.

The young attorney Richard Nixon and his bride to be Pat Ryan celebrate their newly acquired marriage license.

Eventually, Ryan agreed to date the determined young man. Two years later, in 1940, the two were married.

World War II

Shortly after the Nixons were married, the United States entered World War II (1941–1945). To help with the war effort, Nixon took a job in the Office of Price Administration (OPA), the government agency that oversaw the rationing of food and rubber goods. It was here that Nixon got his first taste of government bureaucracy, and he hated it. He was frustrated by the department's inefficiency. The amount of paper work it took to accomplish a simple task disgusted him.

When the call went out for lawyers to serve as officers in the military, Nixon left the OPA and joined the U.S. Navy. He spent most of his time as a naval officer in the Pacific overseeing the distribution of cargo.

Those who knew Nixon during his navy days remember him as the operator of Nick's Hamburger Stand. At this shack, Nick Nixon, as he was called, would serve free hamburgers and drinks to flyers returning from battle. Although Nixon saw little combat, his time in the navy gave him the chance to meet people from all over the United States.

During World War II, Nixon (third from left) was stationed in the South Pacific, serving as a Navy Lieutenant.

After the war, a Republican organization from Whittier was looking for a local candidate and a new face to run for the House of Representatives. Impressed with his credentials as a law-school graduate and a naval officer, a member of this group asked Nixon if he was interested in politics. Richard and Pat realized that campaigning would be expensive; it would wipe out the $10,000 they had saved to buy a house. There was certainly no guarantee that this "new face" would win, but they decided to take the risk.

A CAREER IN POLITICS

*J*erry Voorhis, Nixon's Democratic opponent in the election of 1946, had served in the House of Representatives for ten years. In addition to winning five elections in a row, Voorhis had recently been voted the most hardworking man in Congress by his peers. Defeating him would not be easy.

Nixon was determined to fight a fierce battle. His strategy going into the campaign was to portray Voorhis as a New Deal Democrat, overly committed to big government social programs. After the rationing of World War II, many Americans were sick of the government interfering with their lives. Nixon's strategy was promising.

As the campaign got under way, Nixon took his attack on Voorhis several steps further. He began to portray him as a Socialist—someone who believes that all wealth and property should be divided up among the people. Although Voorhis had briefly joined a socialist organization when he was a young man, he had long since renounced socialism. By 1946 his beliefs placed him squarely in the mainstream of the Democratic Party. However, Nixon decided to imply that if Voorhis was a Socialist once he must still be a Socialist; Voorhis must therefore be sympathetic with the nation's dreaded socialist enemies, the Communists of the Soviet Union.

Nixon got a break when Voorhis agreed to a series of debates. Voorhis had no idea how skilled a debater Nixon was—or how aggressive he would be. In the first debate, Nixon shocked Voorhis by accusing him of taking support from a communist political action committee (PAC). Nixon was blurring the facts. A communist PAC had contributed to a Voorhis campaign years ago, and a PAC with a similar sounding name had sent a contribution to Voorhis recently. But Nixon did not give listeners a chance to consider such subtle distinctions. He continued hurling accusations at Voorhis and kept his opponent on the defensive.

This tactic won Nixon attention in the debates, and he stuck with it throughout the campaign. Day after day he accused Voorhis of being soft on communism. It paid off. On election day the results were not even close. Voorhis was through with politics, and Nixon was elected to the House of Representatives.

Before he became a congressman, Nixon became a father. In early 1946, Pat gave birth to their daughter Tricia. As 1946 drew

Richard, Pat, and baby Tricia Nixon enjoy a spring day in Washington.

to a close, the family of three moved across the country to Washington, D.C., where Nixon would begin his career in politics.

The House of Representatives

In his first year in Congress, Nixon joined the House Committee on Un-American Activities, a group dedicated to identifying Communists. While serving on this committee, Nixon became involved in the case that would boost him to fame: the case of Alger Hiss. Hiss was a highly respected state department official who had served various Democratic administrations. He stood accused of passing secrets to communist agents. His accuser, Whittacker Chambers, was a confessed traitor. Almost no one trusted Chambers—except Richard Nixon.

Other committee members were willing to give up on the

Alger Hiss at the House Committee on Un-American Activities hearings.

case, but Nixon was determined to keep it alive. He put Hiss through several rounds of intense questioning, forcing him to be specific and thorough about what he did or did not do. Eventually, Nixon's investigation led to new evidence. Microfilmed documents found in a hollowed-out pumpkin seemed to support Chambers's story of how Hiss passed secrets to Communists. Disagreement about Hiss's guilt persists to this day, but Nixon managed to convince a jury that Hiss had lied. Hiss was sentenced to prison.

The idea that a trusted government official could be a Communist, horrified many Americans. Some began to fear that Communists were everywhere, trying to deprive Americans of their most basic personal freedoms. By overseeing the conviction of Hiss, Nixon became a hero to these Americans. Nixon also became the enemy of many **liberals**, who believed Nixon had ruined the reputation of an innocent man. Supporters of Hiss were in the minority, but their hatred for Nixon would last.

In 1948 Nixon was reelected to the House. Along with his second victory came his and Pat's second child, Julie. Riding a wave of popularity, Nixon set his sights even higher. He decided to make a run for the U.S. Senate in the 1950 elections.

Nixon's opponent in this race was Helen Gahagan Douglas, a former actress and singer who was seeking reelection as senator from California. Using the same strategy he had used to beat Voorhis, Nixon repeatedly accused Douglas of being soft on communism. Since communism is symbolized by the color red, Nixon labeled Douglas the Pink Lady and claimed she was "pink right down to her underwear." Douglas in turn labeled Nixon Tricky Dick, and with good reason. Throughout the campaign, Nixon supporters used political dirty tricks to turn voters against Douglas. One group made phony postcards which claimed to be from a communist group that expressed support for Douglas. After Nixon defeated Douglas, she was out of politics for good, and he was on his way to the Senate.

Congresswoman Helen Gahagan Douglas was Nixon's opponent during the 1950 senate race.

THE RED MENACE

The definition of communism does little to suggest how that single word inspired such fear in the hearts of Americans throughout most of the twentieth century. In 1917, when the Soviet Union became the world's first communist nation, its leaders seized private property and factories and tried to make sure that the hungriest people were fed. During the Great Depression of the 1930s, when record numbers of Americans were homeless and hungry, many Americans wondered whether communism might be a better form of government than democracy. When the Depression passed, communism became less popular in the United States.

A few years later, World War II left Americans feeling disgusted with governments that limited individual freedoms, as Adolf Hitler and the fascists had done. Soviet leaders were depriving their own citizens of basic human rights and using their military might to bully neighboring nations. Americans came to see communism as a threat to their way of life.

Richard Nixon's ability to tap into American fears made him perfectly suited to the political climate of the day. As he pursued his career as an anti-communist, events overseas played right into his hand. For example, as Nixon was prosecuting Alger Hiss, British leader Winston Churchill announced that the Soviets were keeping the people of Eastern Europe trapped behind an "iron curtain." Meanwhile, in China, Communists led by Mao Zedong were rising up to overthrow the government. These events increased fear of Communists across America.

As Nixon was running for the Senate, almost all of China had fallen to communism. China's Communist neighbor, North Korea, had invaded democratic South Korea. Even worse, the Soviets had built their own atomic bomb; now they could destroy entire cities in seconds. Convinced that Communists everywhere had teamed up to take over the world, Americans were nearly hysterical with fear. Since Nixon was seen as a leading foe of these overseas aggressors, he was nearly unbeatable.

In the Senate

While in the Senate, Nixon used his new visibility to establish himself as a leading speaker for Republican causes and candidates. As his power in the party grew, he found himself positioned to move up yet again. Democrats had held the White House for twenty years, but Republicans were optimistic as the 1952 elections approached. With popular World War II general Dwight "Ike" Eisenhower as their presidential nominee, Republicans believed that they could not lose. Eisenhower's only possible shortcomings were his lack of government experience and his age—at sixty-two he would be the oldest president yet elected. Republicans decided to balance the ticket with a vice-presidential candidate who had both government experience and youth. No one fit that description better than Republican rising star Richard Nixon.

Eisenhower was delighted at the prospect of having Nixon as his vice president. Early in the campaign he had reason to question the choice, however, when it was revealed that Nixon had a **slush fund** of secret contributions from rich donors. Nixon claimed he was using the money to cover political expenses, such as campaign materials and trips, as opposed to personal expenses, such as fancy coats and vacations. To many people the fund seemed improper, as though Nixon was being bribed. Since Eisenhower had been accusing White House Democrats of corruption, he felt his vice-presidential candidate had to be "clean as a hound's tooth."

Rather than end his candidacy, Nixon decided to make a bold move: he would plead his case to the nation on television. At the time, television was new to the American way of life. Most American homes had a single TV set that broadcast a few shows.

Americans were used to seeing situation comedies, game shows, or variety shows on their new TV. Never before had they seen a politician appear live to try to save his career.

"My fellow Americans," Nixon began, "I come before you tonight as a candidate for the vice presidency and as a man whose honesty and integrity have been questioned." With Pat at his side,

U.S. Senator Richard Nixon, Dwight D. Eisenhower, and their wives attend the Republican convention in Chicago 1952.

Nixon went on to give a full account of his expenses to show that he had not used a cent of the slush-fund money for personal items.

A half-hour discussion of one man's finances might be dry and boring, but Nixon used his acting skills to give his presentation personality and heart. He talked about how Pat did not need a mink coat, but was proud to wear a "respectable Republican cloth coat." Then he revealed that over the course of the campaign he had received "a little cocker spaniel dog . . . black and white spotted. And our little girl, Tricia, the six-year-old, named it Checkers. And you know the kids love that dog and I just want to say this right now, that regardless of what they say about it we are going to keep it." Critics thought Nixon's speech

Richard Nixon appeared on TV screens across the nation to make his famous Checkers speech. Wife Pat looks on.

was melodramatic and silly, but most Americans were completely engaged and convinced. Nixon won back the support of the nation and stayed in the race.

Eisenhower's Democratic opponent in the election was Senator Adlai Stevenson of Illinois. Throughout the campaign, Nixon launched verbal attacks at Stevenson so that Eishenhower could appear to be above the fray. Nixon called Stevenson Adlai the appeaser, and accused him of having studied at the College of Cowardly Containment. An appeaser was someone who gave in to Communists, and **containment** was a method of putting up with Communists. Thus, Nixon was again accusing an opponent of being soft on communism. Again, it worked. Eisenhower won the election decisively. After only six years in politics, Richard Nixon would be vice president of the United States.

*I*n the army, Dwight Eisenhower had been excellent at delegating responsibility to other officers. In the White House, Eisenhower also proved willing to delegate, especially to his vice president. Although at thirty-nine years old Nixon was the second-youngest man to become vice president, Eisenhower gave Nixon more responsibility than any vice president had ever had. Over the course of his vice presidency, Nixon was asked to attend nearly two hundred cabinet meetings and over two hundred National Security Council meetings. In dozens of these high-level meetings, Nixon was given the special responsibility of serving as chairman. Eisenhower also sent Nixon abroad on official trips to meet with foreign leaders in fifty-eight different countries. In 1956 the team of Eisenhower and Nixon ran for reelection. Again their opponent was Adlai Stevenson, and again they were victorious.

In his second term as vice president, Nixon found himself in several conflicts that tested his will and courage. In 1957, while on a trip to Ghana, Nixon met the Reverend Martin Luther King Jr. and invited the civil rights leader to visit the White

Richard Nixon invited the Reverend Martin Luther King Jr. to the White House in 1957.

House. When King accepted Nixon's invitation, white southerners were angry; in those days African Americans were rarely
honored with official invitations to the White House. Nixon
defended King's visit. He insisted that Americans could not claim
to have a fairer system of government than the Communists
while repressing an entire race of people.

The following year, while on a goodwill tour of eight Latin
American countries, Nixon encountered anti-American protestors
who stood the term goodwill on its head. In Lima, the capital of
Peru, an angry mob threw stones and spit on Nixon and his
entourage. In the scuffle, Nixon kicked a protestor. In the Venezuelan capital of Caracas, Nixon faced a more serious threat. As
protestors surrounded Nixon's limousine and smashed it with
rocks, pipes, and clubs, a Secret Service agent sitting beside
Nixon took out his gun to shoot at the mob. Nixon ordered the
agent to hold his fire, and
eventually Venezuelan troops
arrived to help the car get free.
This threat on the life of the
vice president made headlines
around the world. Returning
home, Nixon found that his
popularity had soared.

In 1959 Nixon traveled to
the Soviet Union to meet
Soviet leader Nikita Khrushchev.
When Khrushchev took Nixon
to an exhibit that featured the
model of an American kitchen,
the two leaders suddenly found

*Anti-American protestors attack Nixon's car
during his May 1958 visit to Venezuela.*

In the "kitchen debate," Richard Nixon and Nikita Krushchev had a war of words.

themselves in an informal, passionate debate. Khrushchev boasted to Nixon that the Soviets were advancing more quickly than the Americans. He warned that within a few years "we will bury you." Nixon argued right back, responding to each charge his host made with a countercharge. At one point, Nixon poked his finger into Khrushchev's chest and said, "You don't know everything." Many Americans watching the "kitchen debate" on television thought Nixon looked like a true leader.

NIXON VERSUS KENNEDY

At the 1960 Republican convention, Nixon was once again selected for his party's national ticket. This time, though, he was asked to succeed Eisenhower as the thirty-fifth president of the United States. His Democratic opponent, Massachusetts senator John Fitzgerald Kennedy, was no stranger to Nixon. The two men had entered Congress in the same year and had established a cordial working relationship. Kennedy's father had even contributed to an early Nixon campaign.

In terms of background and personal style, there were sharp differences between Nixon and Kennedy. While Nixon's parents had to struggle to keep food on the table, Kennedy belonged to one of the country's most rich and powerful families. While Nixon's long nose and physical awkwardness were often parodied, Kennedy was considered handsome and athletic. Kennedy was Catholic, which was thought to be a disadvantage since no Catholic had ever been elected president. Nixon decided it would be wise to avoid making religion an issue in the election. Instead he chose to focus on Kennedy's relative inexperience. Although at forty-seven, Nixon was himself somewhat young for a presidential candidate, Kennedy was even younger at forty-three. More important, while Kennedy had stayed in Congress, Nixon had spent two terms as vice president, meeting foreign leaders and standing in for the president.

John F. Kennedy thrills a crowd during his run for the presidency in 1960.

DAUGHTERS OF DESTINY

As Richard Nixon worked his way up the political ladder, he began to set his sights on the White House. So did his daughters. At a celebration for the Eisenhower-Nixon team's second inauguration, President Eisenhower's wife Mamie found Julie Nixon in tears. When Mamie asked Julie why she was crying, the eight-year-old replied that it didn't seem fair that the president's grandchildren could play in the White House while she and Tricia couldn't. So Mamie invited Tricia and Julie to join her grandchildren, David, Anne, and Susie Eisenhower, for a play date in the White House.

Tricia (right) and Julie would have far more access to the White House a decade later, when their parents became its official occupants. Tricia lived there until 1971, when she married Edward Cox in a lavish White House wedding. Julie frequently visited the White House with the man she married in 1968—none other than David Eisenhower, the grandson of Dwight Eisenhower who had led her romping around the White House years earlier.

The Campaign of 1960

Although the presidential candidates agreed on major goals, they disagreed about how to achieve them. Kennedy believed the government should give money directly to public schools to help pay teachers' salaries. Nixon believed the government should help schools by lending the states money for school construction. Kennedy favored the Housing Act of 1960, which called for the government to build 810,000 low-rent public housing units in six years. Nixon called this act socialistic and opposed it. Both candidates wanted to stop the spread of communism, but Kennedy accused Nixon of being trigger-happy, while Nixon once again accused his opponent of appeasement.

Nixon was no stranger to campaigning, but the pressures of running for president took a far greater toll than his earlier campaigns had. One day, while working his way through a noisy crowd, Nixon bumped his knee against a car door and received an injury that would not go away. Days later, doctors told Nixon that the knee had become dangerously infected. For two weeks Nixon lay in a hospital bed recovering as Kennedy was shaking hands and winning votes.

Another disappointment for Nixon was Eisenhower's half-hearted support. When reporters asked Eisenhower to give an example of a major policy decision to which Nixon had contributed, the popular president responded, "If you give me a week I might think of one." Later Eisenhower said he had been joking and apologized to Nixon, but the damage had been done.

A dramatic highlight of the 1960 campaign was the first-ever televised debates between presidential candidates. Given his experience as a debater and his successful use of television in his Checkers speech, Nixon had cause to believe that the debates would serve him well against Kennedy. As the first debate approached, however, Nixon was ill with a high fever and still recovering from the ordeal with his knee. As a result, he appeared thin, pale, and worn out. On the other hand, Kennedy looked hardy and tanned. Nixon's haggard looks did not affect his debating skill; a slight majority of those listening on the radio believed Nixon had won. But millions more had watched the debates on television. To them Kennedy appeared far more presidential.

As election day neared, pollsters predicted that the vote would be extremely close, and it was. The popular vote was the

Republican vice president Richard Nixon listens to Senator John F. Kennedy, the Democratic presidential nominee, during their fourth debate on October 21, 1960.

closest yet in American history. Kennedy ended up with 49.71 percent of the vote to Nixon's 49.55. Even though Kennedy won the electoral vote by a wider margin, a shift of a few thousand votes in two states could have given the presidency to Nixon. When there were reports of voter fraud in Texas and Illinois, Eisenhower and other Republican leaders urged Nixon to call for a recount. Nixon decided against this course of action, since a recount could have taken years and divided the country. So, when his term as vice president ended, Nixon suddenly found himself without a job.

THE NEW NIXON

*U*pon his return to California, Nixon wrote about the most dramatic challenges he had faced during his career in *Six Crises* (1962). Then, after writing about history, Nixon yearned to get back to making history. In September 1961 he announced that he would run for governor of California in the 1962 election.

Nixon's Democratic opponent in this race, incumbent governor Pat Brown, turned out to be as aggressive as Nixon had been against Voorhis and Douglas. Brown attacked Nixon for associating with the extremely conservative John Birch Society, as Nixon had attacked Voorhis for having associated with Socialists. He accused Nixon of aiming to use the California statehouse as a stepping stone to the White House, for which Brown claimed Nixon would surely run in 1964. Nixon also had to defend himself against the charge that he had been bribed by the Hughes Tool Company, which had loaned money to his brother while Nixon was vice president. Nixon tried to focus on issues, but they played little role in this election. As he would later write, "Most reporters showed little interest in the . . . proposals I made on the cost of state government, crime, education, or . . . creating a better business climate in California."

At the end of a tough, nasty fight, Nixon lost by a considerable margin. Barely losing the presidency had been painful, but being soundly defeated for the governorship of his home state was humiliating. In a post-election press conference, Nixon lashed out at the press. He taunted that in future elections they should "put one lonely reporter on the campaign who will report

Defeated gubernatorial candidate Richard Nixon tells the press, "You won't have Nixon to kick around anymore . . ."

what the candidate says now and then." Then he shocked listeners by announcing, "You won't have Nixon to kick around anymore because, gentlemen, this is my last press conference." Exhausted and fed up, Richard Nixon seemed to be saying goodbye to politics. The television network ABC aired a documentary special called *The Political Obituary of Richard Nixon*. With Nixon now looking like a loser, his political life appeared to have come to an end.

THE COMEBACK

While most Americans accepted that Nixon was finished, Nixon himself never did. Over the coming months, he would begin one of the most amazing political comebacks in American history.

AMERICA'S LONGEST WAR

Lasting from 1957 to 1975, the Vietnam War is considered America's longest war. For the people of Vietnam the conflict was even longer, having started over a decade earlier when communist rebels led by Ho Chi Minh rose up against the French-backed government. Although the rebels saw their struggle as a fight for independence from foreign rule, American leaders saw it as an attempt to spread communism through Southeast Asia. Determined to oppose communism everywhere in the world, President Harry Truman sent military advisors and funds to help the French crush the rebels in the early 1950s.

In spite of American support, the French Army was forced to surrender in 1954. When the French departed, Vietnam was divided in half,

with a communist government led by Ho Chi Minh in the North and an anticommunist government in the South. Though an election was to be held to determine which government would control the entire nation, this election never took place. Instead, the government of South Vietnam declared its intent to be a permanent nation, independent of the North.

Unwilling to leave the nation divided, the Communists began a series of attacks against the South Vietnamese government. Eisenhower provided funds and advisors to support the South Vietnamese Army, and Kennedy greatly increased both forms of military support, but the communists continued to make headway.

Shortly after President Johnson took office in 1964, an American destroyer allegedly got into a skirmish with North Vietnamese torpedo boats in the Gulf of Tonkin off the coast of North Vietnam. Provoked by this news, Congress authorized Johnson to escalate the U.S. role in the war. Over the next four years, Johnson sent increasing numbers of American troops to fight in Vietnam until they numbered over half a million. He also sent American planes to bomb selected targets in North Vietnam.

Johnson repeatedly assured Americans that the war was being won, but the Communists never seemed to weaken. In the Tet Offensive of 1968, communist **guerrillas** launched a series of attacks on urban areas throughout South Vietnam. This act included overtaking the U.S. embassy in the South Vietnamese capital of Saigon. The Communists were removed from the embassy and other cities they had attacked, but they had achieved a public-relations victory. As a result, Americans came to think that the mighty United States could not win this war.

His reentry into politics would be a gradual one, made up of a series of careful steps.

In the 1964 presidential election, Nixon found a way to gain power by *not* running. Months before the campaign began, in fall 1963, President Kennedy had been assassinated in Dallas. His successor, Lyndon Baines Johnson, inherited Kennedy's popularity. As Johnson campaigned to keep the presidency, polls showed him way ahead of his Republican opponent, Barry Goldwater, a controversial conservative Arizona senator. Goldwater seemed so certain to lose that many prominent Republicans did not even bother to campaign for him. Nixon, however, resolved to stand up for his party. He made 150 appearances in thirty-six states to campaign for Goldwater and other Republican candidates. As expected, Goldwater lost in a landslide, but Nixon's spirit made him a hero in the eyes of Republicans.

Over the next two years, Nixon continued to inch back into the spotlight. Crossing the country to raise funds for the party, he appeared before six hundred groups in forty states. He put together a campaign staff and wrote articles criticizing Johnson's foreign policy. In the elections of 1966, he campaigned for Republican candidates again, and helped the party make major gains in Congress. By this point, Republican governors, senators, and representatives across the country owed their jobs, in part, to Nixon's support. Soon he would be calling on them to return the favor.

THE ELECTION OF 1968

The year 1968 proved to be the perfect time for Nixon to return to center stage of the American political scene. It was a turbulent year, marked by bold styles and loud music. Many high-school and college students defied social norms and experimented with

A riot breaks out in Chicago between demonstrators and police outside the Federal Building, where eight persons were on trial for promoting riots during the 1968 Democratic National Convention.

drugs, hairstyles, and alternative lifestyles. Members of various minority groups were speaking out for their rights and often took to the streets to protest discrimination. President Johnson's ambitious Great Society programs, though designed to help the poor, created intense disappointment and anger. The assassination of Martin Luther King Jr. by white racist James Earl Ray ignited race riots across the country.

As the Vietnam War dragged on, the nation was dividing into **doves** who believed the United States should pull out of Vietnam and **hawks** who believed Americans should stay and fight even harder. The tensions between hawks and doves, black and white, rich and poor, and young and old had never seemed more explosive.

Amid all the noise, Nixon realized that he would do well to position himself as a **moderate**. In past elections he had stirred

Richard Nixon and Spiro Agnew wave to the crowd after receiving their party's nomination at the 1968 Republican National Convention.

fear of communism, antagonized liberals, and provoked the press. This time he was determined to be different. While extremists on both sides attacked one another, he would appear as a sane, calming influence, speaking for the many Americans who were tired of the national strife.

As the Republican National Convention approached, Nixon carefully adjusted his position on civil rights so he would appeal to the majority of his party. Since his past support for civil rights had made some Republicans fear he was too liberal, now Nixon made a point of reaching out to conservative white southerners. These southerners were angry at the Supreme Court for ordering southern state universities to be desegregated. To please them Nixon promised that if elected he would nominate conservative judges to the court.

After winning the support of conservative Republicans, Nixon won his party's nomination for president. He picked Maryland governor Spiro Agnew as his running mate. Critics mocked Nixon's choice of the relatively unknown governor, but Nixon believed he had found a qualified man who would not offend any segment of the party.

While the Republicans used their convention to unify, the Democrats used theirs to self-destruct. Johnson had dropped out of the race after his handling of the Vietnam War had caused his popularity to plummet. In his absence, Vice President Hubert Humphrey became the leading Democratic candidate. As Humphrey defended Johnson's hawkish role in the war, he was fiercely opposed by the leading Democratic dove, Minnesota senator Eugene McCarthy. On the convention floor, hawks battled doves with angry speeches and jeers. Meanwhile, outside the convention hall, police battled antiwar protestors

Outside the Democratic Convention a police officer handcuffs a demonstrator.

with clubs and teargas. People watching the convention on TV saw images of Humphrey's joyous victory alternating with images of chaos and bloodshed.

The Democrats were further weakened by the campaign of Alabama governor George Wallace, who had left the Democratic Party to run as a third-party candidate. As the segregationist Wallace stirred anger against northern liberals, and the Democrats presented a picture of dissent and disarray, Nixon's calm, reasonable persona became even more welcome. Columnist Walter Lippmann observed that there appeared to be "a new Nixon, a maturer and mellower man who is no longer clawing his way to the top . . . who has outlived and outgrown the ruthless politics of his early days."

To preserve this image, Nixon ran his presidential campaign like an advertising campaign, focusing on image rather than ideas. Unhappy with the way reporters had portrayed him in the past, Nixon avoided interviews. Also unhappy with the way the debates against Kennedy had turned out, he avoided debates. Instead, Nixon allowed the TV-viewing public to see him in town-hall meetings that appeared to be spontaneous, but were carefully scripted. One journalist complained that Nixon was a "cardboard candidate" about whom "we don't know a thing."

One of the few issues Nixon did emphasize in his campaign was the vague promise to restore "law and order." This had never been used in a national campaign before, since law enforcement is normally the responsibility of local police and not the federal government. But Nixon's praise of law and order showed that he was opposed to the riots, racial unrest, and social upheaval of the day.

As far as the Vietnam War was concerned, Nixon claimed he had a plan to end it, but insisted that he could not discuss his plan. Nixon had indeed promised Johnson that he would not interfere with the delicate peace negotiations underway by criticizing the president's handling of the war. The main reason Nixon did

During the campaign of 1968, Richard Nixon began to seem, once again, like a winner.

not reveal his plan was political, however. By not being specific, he could avoid alienating voters on either side of this polarizing issue.

Nixon began the race with a sizable lead in the polls, but Humphrey steadily gained ground as he distanced himself from Johnson. When Johnson stopped the bombing of North Vietnam as a step toward peace negotiations, Humphrey closed in even further. But when last-minute peace negotiations broke down, Americans voted for a change and elected Nixon.

In terms of the popular vote, Nixon's margin of victory was extremely slim. Having lost a close election before though, Nixon was pleased to announce in his victory speech, "Winning's a lot more fun!" Then Nixon pledged to honor a sign he had seen while campaigning, which implored him to BRING US TOGETHER.

PRESIDENT NIXON AND DOMESTIC ISSUES

After finally completing his long journey to the presidency, Richard Nixon found himself with surprisingly little power. Even though voters had elected a Republican president, they had left both the Senate and the House of Representatives with Democratic majorities. The first president in 120 years to take office with both houses of Congress controlled by the opposing party, he would not have an easy time getting bills passed.

To make the best use of his power, Nixon organized his staff in a unique way. In particular, he believed that keeping his inner circle as small as possible would allow him to govern more effectively. Among those in Nixon's innermost circle was Chief of Staff Bob Haldeman. "I'm his buffer," Haldeman said of Nixon. Haldeman did indeed function as a kind of shock absorber, protecting Nixon from aggravations and distractions of every kind.

Another of Nixon's most trusted confidants was John Ehrlichman, who began as assistant for domestic affairs and soon took charge of the Domestic

Bob Haldeman (left) and John Ehrlichman were among President Nixon's closest advisors.

Affairs Council. Ehrlichman had been friends with Haldeman since college, and they worked together perfectly. Both men were extremely religious and hardworking. Together, Haldeman and Ehrlichman controlled the flow of information to the president.

Nixon's other closest advisors on domestic issues included Professor Daniel Patrick Moynihan, a liberal, and economist Arthur F. Burns, a conservative. Although the president wanted to limit the information that reached him, he was eager to hear it from different points of view.

Realizing the need for public support in his battles with Congress, Nixon kept a public-relations staff working full time to help him understand and control public opinion. Nixon saw members of the press as his enemies, and he did not intend to let them defeat his plans. He made sure that his public-relations team released just the right information to the media at just the right moment.

PROTECTING THE ENVIRONMENT

As president, one issue that Nixon chose to act upon was the environment. Air pollution was not new, but it was just beginning to get the attention of people across the country. Americans had become alarmed that the Great Lakes were turning green and smelling foul, that the air was being polluted by cars and factories, and that forests were being chopped down to make room for parking lots and shopping malls.

Working with Congress, Nixon established the Environmental Protection Agency to oversee all government agencies that dealt with pollution. He expanded the National Park Service and oversaw the nation's first Earth Day celebration in 1971. He signed into law the Clean Air Act and the Water Pollution Control Act, which limit the amounts of certain chemicals that businesses, power plants, and cars may release into the air and water. While today's Republicans tend to favor the concerns of business over the environment, Nixon took a middle road. He did not try to eliminate corporate pollution, but he attempted to limit it whenever possible.

Nixon's record of federal support for the arts also differs from today's Republicans. While Presidents Kennedy and Johnson increased government spending for the arts, Nixon topped them both. His commitment to the arts was not only political, but also personal. Nixon had loved the theater since his acting days in school, and he had always had a special passion for music. One of his greatest thrills in the White House was hosting a seventieth birthday party for jazz legend Duke Ellington. Nixon himself played "Happy Birthday" for the Duke on the piano.

The nation got an emotional lift on the evening of July 20, 1969, when American astronaut Neil Armstrong became the first person to walk on the moon. After that historic moment, Nixon spoke by phone to Armstrong and the other astronauts who had made the journey. He told them that the thoughts of all the world were with them and he was hardly exaggerating; 528 million people around the world had been watching the astronauts on TV. As Americans beheld the amazing feats their nation could achieve in space, many wondered why more could not be done to help people closer to home.

A great supporter of the arts, Richard Nixon hosted the seventieth birthday party for jazz great Duke Ellington.

Fighting Poverty

Nixon himself had been thinking along those lines, but he sought to help the poor in a different way than his predecessors had. Ever since President Franklin Delano Roosevelt set up his New Deal social programs to help the poor, presidents had tried to end poverty by using government programs. Kennedy's New Frontier and Johnson's Great Society were the two most recent examples. Nixon explained his problem with this approach in his notes to a speechwriter:

I remember when my brother had tuberculosis . . . and we had to keep him in the hospital, my mother didn't buy a new dress for five years. We were really quite desperately poor, but . . . we didn't know it. The problem today is that children growing up in welfare families receiving food stamps . . . with social workers poking around are poor and they do know it. This is our chance now to see that every child will grow up with some degree of pride.

Nixon had two main plans to help the poor in ways he felt would preserve their pride. The first was called a **negative income tax**. Under this plan, instead of paying taxes, the poorest Americans would receive payments from the government to help pay for basic necessities. His other plan was called **revenue sharing**. This meant that instead of spending money on social programs, the federal government would pass money directly to officials in state and local governments who would see that funds reached those who needed them most. Nixon had trouble getting these plans passed by Congress, but a revenue-sharing bill was finally passed in 1972. His efforts to combat poverty were not as widely celebrated as Johnson's Great Society programs had been, but under Nixon the government spent more money on the poor than it had under Johnson.

Nixon also took steps to help improve the lives of African Americans—while being careful to avoid upsetting his conservative southern white supporters. Early in the term, Nixon's attorney general, John Mitchell, told a group of African Americans, "You would be well advised to watch what we do rather than what we say." Mitchell's words proved true. While managing to appear moderate or even conservative on race relations, Nixon doubled the budget for aid to black colleges, increased the budget for enforcing civil rights laws by 800 percent, and increased the number of blacks in government by 37 percent. Nixon's progress on race relations was not well publicized, but it was real.

President Nixon meets his African-American administration appointees.

Pat Nixon in the Nation's Service

Although Pat Nixon did not care for politics, she had a deep passion for public service. While serving as first lady she championed volunteerism, the idea that people should help one another instead of relying on government. Pat made more than 150 trips to different parts of the country to honor volunteers for their service and to lend her support to programs like the Right to Read program, which empowered people to help themselves. When she was not honoring or empowering people across the country, Pat was entertaining them in the White House. In the second year of the Nixon presidency, she welcomed a record 50,000 guests.

When the Nixons were living in New York in the mid-1960s, their elevator operator mentioned to Pat that he had never visited a national park because he could not afford to travel to one. First Lady Pat remembered the elevator operator's words and took action. She helped to set up the Legacy of the Parks Program, which brought small parks to major cities so poor people could afford to visit.

Besides helping out with domestic problems, Pat served her nation in frequent trips abroad. In 1970 she brought urgently needed supplies and organized volunteers to Peru, which had been devastated by an earthquake. And in 1972, by attending the inauguration of the president of Liberia, she became the first first lady to represent the United States on an official international mission.

The most inflammatory racial issue of the day was busing, a method of desegregating public schools by sending children to schools outside their neighborhood. When Nixon took office, public schools throughout the south and in parts of the north were filled with children of only one race. The Supreme Court's 1954 ruling in *Brown v. Board of Education*, which ordered that public schools be integrated "with all deliberate speed," had brought about little change. In 1969 the court decided that "all deliberate speed" was not good enough; schools had to be desegregated at once.

Nixon thought busing was a bad idea. When the Supreme Court ordered busing, however, he was determined to see it carried out. In parts of the country, resistance sometimes became

The Berkeley, California school district was one of the first to voluntarily desegregate using busing.

violent. Nixon saw to it that the law was observed. For the first time in U.S. history, black and white children across the country began going to school together. Early in the 1970 school year, Pat Moynihan proudly announced, "There has been more change in the structure of American public school education in the past month than in the past one hundred years."

As public education moved in a direction that pleased Liberals, Nixon was eager to please Conservatives by making good on his campaign promise to put Conservatives on the Supreme Court. Fulfilling this promise would not be easy though. When Nixon nominated Judge Clement F. Haynsworth Jr. of South Carolina to replace Justice Abe Fortas, Democrats in Congress protested. Seeking revenge against Republicans who had forced Fortas to step down, Democrats pointed out two cases in which Haynsworth had shown questionable judgment. Then they used those cases to gather momentum against Haynsworth's nomination.

Nixon could have avoided a fight by withdrawing the nomination, but he decided that backing down would encourage members of Congress to overrule him again. He had to show them "you can't kick Nixon!" So the president dug in his heels and battled for his nominee, who lost anyway.

Then, as if to punish the Democrats who had opposed Haynsworth, Nixon nominated a judge who was even more conservative and even more southern, Judge G. Harrold Carswell of Florida. Unfortunately for Nixon, the staff members who recommended Carswell had not done their homework. A look at Carswell's record revealed that he was a segregationist. Besides belonging to a country club that excluded blacks, in the 1940s he had said whites were better than blacks. Since then, he had not publicly expressed a change of heart.

Once again Nixon dug in his heels, and once again his nominee was defeated. In disgust, Nixon claimed it was impossible to get a southern judge on the Supreme Court as long as Democrats controlled Congress. Having two nominations in a row defeated was a blow to the president's prestige. But it was also a kind of victory for Nixon. He had come off as a fighter for the cause of white southerners, who would continue to support him to the end.

Having given up on nominating a southerner, Nixon nominated Harry Blackmun of Minnesota who was readily approved by

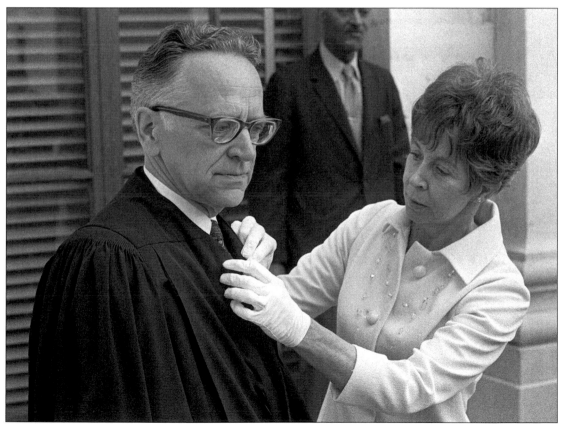

Supreme Court Justice Harry Blackmun after taking oath to join the high court on June 9, 1970.

Congress. Over the course of his presidency, Nixon put four judges on the Supreme Court: Blackmun; Warren Burger, who served as chief justice; William Rehnquist, who would later serve as chief justice; and Lewis F. Powell Jr. Filling nearly half the court's nine seats, these justices did make the court more conservative than it had been. They put an end to forced busing, for example. However, the court did not become as conservative as some might have expected. It was Blackmun who wrote the opinion on the case *Roe v. Wade*, which legalized abortion. Conservatives have long opposed this ruling.

As Nixon struggled to find a balance between making social progress and appeasing Conservatives at home, he was getting far more attention—and facing even greater challenges—in foreign affairs.

PRESIDENT NIXON AND INTERNATIONAL ISSUES

Six

𝓘n his inaugural speech on January 20, 1969, Nixon proclaimed that "the greatest honor history can bestow is the title of peacemaker." One of his goals as president was to earn that title. Although Nixon had spent years establishing a reputation as the leading enemy of Communists, by the time of his presidency, he believed in a less warlike approach to dealing with communist nations. This approach was called **détente**.

PEACE WITH HONOR

Nixon was determined to ease tension with the Communists in Vietnam. During the campaign, he had spoken of a secret plan for ending the war. Now Americans and others around the world were anxious to see what that plan was. Privately, Nixon believed that an American victory was not possible; forcing the North Vietnamese to surrender would require the use of nuclear weapons or bombing North Vietnam's dikes. Nixon himself favored these aggressive methods, but he realized that the American public would not tolerate them. Accepting that the United States could not win the war, Nixon wanted to reach a settlement that would allow the United States to appear strong and still able to honor its commitments to democracies around the world. Nixon referred to this sort of settlement as peace with honor.

A key part of Nixon's plan to bring peace with honor was **Vietnamization**, the process by which the South Vietnamese

55

The June 20, 1969 issue of Time *magazine announces U.S. troop withdrawl from Vietnam.*

would be trained to defend themselves as American troops were gradually withdrawn. In the spring of 1969, Nixon called for both North Vietnamese and American troops to leave South Vietnam and withdrew 25,000 of the 550,000 American troops.

Nixon believed these troop withdrawals would appease the American public. But as soldiers returned home, they brought reports that gave the public cause for increased concern. Americans were distressed to learn that the morale of their troops in Vietnam was deteriorating, and that many soldiers were dealing with their despair by turning to drugs. Even more alarming were reports that South Vietnam's president Nguyen Van Thieu had imprisoned some 80,000 of his own citizens.

As frustration with the war grew, Congress began passing bills that would force the president to remove all troops by a certain time. Americans began protesting in record numbers. On October 15, 1969, opponents of the war held a **moratorium**. The protests went beyond college campuses and into the cities and towns of America. Some 250,000 people marched on Washington, D.C., as people across the country wore black armbands to show their opposition to the war.

In response to the moratorium, Nixon gave a speech in which he said that most Americans quietly supported U.S. involvement in the war. This "silent majority" of Americans, Nixon claimed, were willing to wait until peace with honor could be achieved. Nixon went on to say that the protestors were hurting the cause of freedom by giving comfort and hope to the North Vietnamese.

As the public continued to clamor for "peace now," Nixon worked to achieve peace with honor. Working closely with him in this effort was his national security advisor Henry Kissinger, a foreign-policy scholar whose ideas about getting tough with Communists appealed to Nixon. While Nixon controlled the

Protestors of the Vietnam War march in Washington, D.C.

Henry Kissinger: Man of the World

Born in Fürth, Germany, in 1923, Henry Kissinger came to the United States in 1938 when his family fled Nazi persecution of the Jews. After graduating from Harvard University, Kissinger became a professor of foreign relations and wrote a book called *Nuclear Weapons and Foreign Policy* (1957), which established him as an expert on defense policy. Over the course of the 1960s, Kissinger was hired to provide advice for presidents Kennedy and Johnson. Then he was appointed national security advisor to Nixon.

Although Nixon had grand foreign policy strategies, he relied on the shrewd and practical Kissinger to develop the tactics by which to carry out his ambitious plans. As Alexander Haig, who served under both men, describes their collaboration,

Kissinger is probably the most astute tactician I have ever worked with. . . . Nixon, on the other hand, is a long-term thinker in the area of foreign policy; Henry is far more pragmatic than Nixon. So they made a very good combination.

In service to Nixon's global vision, Kissinger arranged a historic meeting with the Communist Chinese, advanced détente with the Soviets, and negotiated the settlement that ended American involve-ment in the Vietnam War. In 1973 his role in that settlement won Kissinger and Le Duc Tho the Nobel Peace Prize. Also in that year, Kissinger became Nixon's secretary of state, the first person to serve in that position who was not born a U.S. citizen.

war effort from the White House, Kissinger went to Paris to begin secret peace talks with North Vietnamese representative Le Duc Tho.

In the spring of 1970 Nixon announced further troop withdrawals, promising that 150,000 more troops would be home by the end of the year. As troops came home, the number of American casualties went down, which helped to calm the public. But later that spring, Nixon made another announcement that caused yet another public uproar: American troops had moved across the Vietnamese border into Cambodia to attack Communist hideouts there. Sending troops into Cambodia was necessary, Nixon

National Guardsmen fire tear gas and bullets into a crowd of demonstrators at Kent State University.

claimed, to prevent the North Vietnamese from passing weapons through Cambodia to Communists in the South. Many Americans believed Nixon was continuing the war at a time when he should be ending it. A new wave of protests hit college campuses.

As some of these protests became passionate, anger led to violence and bloodshed. During a protest at Kent State University in Ohio on May 4, 1970, four students were killed by National Guardsmen. Ten days later, at Jackson State University in Mississippi, two students were killed during antiwar protests. The violence against protesters only inspired more protests. That spring nine hundred colleges and universities across the country closed for student or faculty strikes. Nixon had to stay away from his daughter Julie's graduation at Smith College for fear of the violent protests his presence would inspire.

As the public outcry against his policies became more shrill, Nixon became quiet. Instead of attacking his opponents directly, he used his vice president to do the name calling, as Eisenhower had used Nixon. Making use of his distinctive vocabulary, Agnew called college students who spoke out against the war "an effete corps of impudent snobs." He called politicians who were against the war "parasites of passion." He called members of the press—all of whom he felt were opposed to the war—"nattering nabobs of negativism." Agnew's alliterative insults got a lot of attention, but they did little to calm the public or to bring Americans together.

THE TRIP TO CHINA

Meanwhile, working in secret, Nixon and Kissinger were plotting a daring move that would throw their communist opponents off balance. Their plan was meant to impact the situation in

Vietnam, but it involved a larger nation slightly to the north. The People's Republic of China, as the communist nation on the Chinese mainland was called, was the most populous country on earth. Yet since its formation over two decades earlier, it had existed in almost complete isolation from the rest of the world. Although the nationalist Chinese in Taiwan had a representative in the United Nations, the far greater nation on the mainland did not. The people of Communist China felt bitter about being excluded from the community of nations.

Nixon had consistently spoken out in favor of supporting nationalist China, while criticizing the Communist Chinese. But by the time of his presidency, Nixon had come to believe that the United States would be wise to establish friendly relations with the large, powerful communist nation. If the United States and China established friendly relations, Nixon believed the friendship would drive a wedge between China and the Soviet Union. With the world's two great communist powers focusing their suspicion on each other, they would be less able to focus on other parts of the world, such as Vietnam.

In 1969, when Chinese and Soviet troops got into a brief border skirmish, Nixon sensed the time was right to begin taking steps toward friendship. He eased trade restrictions to allow the Chinese to sell their goods in the United States. He allowed the American Ping-Pong team to go to China to play the Chinese team. And he began laying the groundwork for a visit that would prove almost as dazzling as Neil Armstrong's visit to the moon. In summer 1971, after two years of delicate, top-secret negotiations, Nixon was finally able to announce that the president of the United States would be making an official trip to Communist China.

The most important moment of the trip was probably the

first, when Nixon stepped off the plane and greeted Chinese premier Chou En-Lai. In 1954 Chou had been deeply hurt when American official John Foster Dulles encountered Chou at a conference in Switzerland and refused to shake his hand. When Nixon stepped off the plane, he went right up to the Chinese premier and shook his hand. As they rode away together, Chou told Nixon, "Your handshake came over the vastest ocean in the world: twenty-five years of no communication."

The rest of the trip featured a series of festive events that provided perfect photo opportunities and superb TV news footage. A highlight was Nixon's meeting with Mao Zedong, the aging visionary who had organized China's communist revolution. Nixon and Mao got along well; Nixon quoted from Mao's writings, and Mao praised Nixon's book *Six Crises*. Nixon's hosts took him to the Great Wall of China, where he announced that he looked forward to a world without walls. He went to a Chinese opera, various athletic events, and parades. Pat was treated to a tour of Chinese schools and hospitals. Everywhere they went, the Nixons were honored and adored by the people of China, who were genuinely touched to be recognized by the American leaders. Overall, the trip was a brilliant move that only Nixon could have made. A president whose reputation as an anti-communist was less secure would likely have been accused of being too friendly with the enemy.

Nixon's trip to China was watched around the world, nowhere more closely than in the Soviet Union. Fearful that China might be teaming up with the United States, the Soviets were now more anxious to deal with Nixon. In May 1972 Nixon headed to the Soviet Union, where he and Soviet premier Leonid Brezhnev discussed plans to limit nuclear arms. Besides these strategic arms limitation talks, the two leaders agreed on a deal by which the United States would sell wheat to the Soviets. They also discussed ways the two nations could work together in space.

President Nixon makes a historic visit to the Great Wall of China.

Even as Nixon was working to improve U.S. relations with the world's two communist superpowers, he put these new friendships to the test. When North Vietnamese troops invaded South Vietnam in spring 1972, Nixon responded by resuming the bombing of North Vietnam. He also mined the North Vietnamese harbor of Haiphong and bombed rail links to China. This made it impossible for the North Vietnamese to get arms and supplies from their Soviet and Chinese allies. Nixon believed that China and the Soviet Union would abandon North Vietnam rather than endanger their new friendships with the United States, and he was right. As the United States increased its efforts to defeat the North Vietnamese, neither the Soviets nor the Chinese rushed to their aid.

THE ELECTION OF 1972

As the presidential election of 1972 approached, Kissinger made a major announcement: he and Le Duc Tho were close to completing a deal that would call for a cease-fire, the withdrawal of American troops, and the return of all American prisoners of war. The timing of his announcement that "peace is within reach," as well as the diplomatic successes with China and the Soviet Union, could not have been better for Nixon.

Earlier in his term, Nixon's chance of being reelected seemed uncertain. The antiwar protests were bitter and strident. His domestic achievements were not well publicized. Since Nixon had barely eked out the election of 1968, he felt he would have to take bold steps to win in 1972. So Nixon had John Mitchell set up the Committee to Reelect the President (CRP) and made it clear that Mitchell should do whatever he had to do to win the election. The sort of dirty tricks Nixon's supporters had used against Helen Gahagan Douglas would be among the tamer measures taken by CRP, which critics mocked with the nickname CREEP.

Nixon's hope for reelection got a break early in his term when tragedy struck Senator Edward Kennedy. The younger brother of the former president, Senator Kennedy had seemed a likely democratic nominee for the 1972 election and Nixon's toughest possible opponent. However, Kennedy's role in the accidental death of Mary Jo Kopechne on Chappaquiddick Island severely damaged his reputation.

When polls showed Democratic senator Ed Muskie of Maine to be Nixon's next leading rival, CRP workers sent out fake mailings that made it seem as though Muskie had insulted Canadians. They also released libelous stories about Muskie's wife to the press. Flustered by these attacks, Muskie broke down in public and dropped out of the race.

CRP continued to take aim at potential Democratic rivals until the Democrats ended up with the candidate whom CRP considered the weakest: George McGovern. A liberal senator who called for immediate withdrawal of American troops from Vietnam, McGovern might have had a chance if opposition to the war had been at its peek. But by the end of 1972, Nixon had convinced Americans that peace with honor was at hand, so he had little reason to fear being defeated by McGovern. After sitting out most of the election, Nixon campaigned only in the final weeks and won by a landslide, carrying every state but Massachusetts.

A POW greets his family upon his return to the United States in 1973.

Shortly after the election, the peace talks between Kissinger and Le Duc Tho broke off. To get the Communists to accept certain terms, Nixon stepped up the bombing of North Vietnam. U.S. troops bombarded the capital city of Hanoi and surrounding areas for eleven days. This Christmas bombing destroyed North Vietnamese power plants, rail yards, airfields, and communication centers, and reduced entire towns to rubble. Though Nixon's critics called the bombing "war by tantrum," the Christmas bombings produced the intended result: the Communists returned to the bargaining table. On January 27, 1973, a formal peace treaty was signed. Within weeks the last American troops had departed from Vietnam and the American prisoners of war were returned. Americans rejoiced at what appeared to be the peace with honor Nixon had promised.

As the troops departed, Nixon guaranteed the leaders of South Vietnam that the American military would return if the North Vietnamese violated the peace treaty. However, Nixon would not be able to keep that promise—or to reach many of the other goals he had set for his second term—because of a botched burglary.

WATERGATE

$\mathcal{T}$he story of the national nightmare known as Watergate involves spying, lying, and stealing by government officials. But the officials who were involved in those crimes saw their actions as a response to a crime that had been committed against them: the release of the Pentagon Papers.

In June 1971 the *New York Times* began printing secret documents that had been prepared for military planners in the Pentagon. These documents revealed startling facts about the war in Vietnam, such as the fact that American leaders had disagreed about whether the war could ever be won. The documents also revealed lies the American people had been told about the war.

Though the Pentagon Papers dealt with actions taken under presidents who came before Nixon, the possibility that top-secret, foreign-policy plans would be leaked to the press infuriated Nixon and Kissinger. Nixon's whole strategy to end the war involved keeping secrets. He believed it was crucial to conceal from the enemy what he was really thinking. At times he had also taken pains to conceal from the American people what he was really doing. For example, the military had bombed Cambodia in secret long before the public found out. Even the planning of the trip to China, which he and Kissinger were pursuing at this time, was being carefully concealed to avoid upsetting Conservatives.

THE PLUMBERS

Determined to keep people from leaking his secrets to the public, Nixon established a special team that was responsible for collecting and protecting confidential information. Many of the men on this team had previous experience spying for the government in such organizations as the Federal Bureau of Investigation (FBI) and the Central Intelligence Agency (CIA). Because one of their main responsibilities would be sealing leaks, this group became known as the Plumbers.

The Plumbers' first assignment was to gather information about Daniel Ellsberg, the man who had released the Pentagon Papers. They broke into the office of Ellsberg's psychiatrist, in the hopes of finding proof that Ellsberg was working for Communists. They ransacked the office, but found no incriminating information about Ellsberg.

For their next mission, the Plumbers set their sights on a more ambitious target: the Democratic National Party's headquarters in Washington, D.C.'s, Watergate Hotel. During the early morning

The Watergate Hotel was the scene of the burglary of the Democratic Party's headquarters, which led to the downfall of President Nixon.

hours of June 17, 1972, the Plumbers broke into the Democrats' headquarters and began snooping around for information that could embarrass Democratic leaders. Amazingly, with all the spying experience some of the Plumbers had, their plans were foiled by a night watchman, Frank Wills. When Wills noticed that a garage door had been tampered with, he called the D.C. police. In no time, seven men involved in the break-in were arrested and jailed.

Officials in the White House called the event a third-rate burglary and denied involvement, but certain details made their denial hard to believe. For one thing, one of the burglars had a phone book with the entree "W. H." and a White House phone number. It turned out that two of the men arrested worked for the CRP.

A pair of young reporters for the *Washington Post*, Robert Woodward and Carl Bernstein, were disturbed by the burglar's connection to the president's campaign staff. They decided to investigate the situation more closely. Woodward and Bernstein questioned countless White House aides and government workers. Many people they approached refused to answer questions. Others, however, provided clues, guidance, and key facts that allowed Woodward and Bernstein to trace the connection between the Watergate burglars and people working in the White House. Administration officials contradicted Woodward and Bernstein's articles and threatened the *Washington Post*, but

Washington Post *reporters Carl Bernstein (left) and Robert Woodward linked the Watergate break-in to the White House.*

the reporters kept investigating and the articles kept coming.

Relatively few Americans shared the *Post*'s concern about Watergate. In fact, at the time of the 1972 election, fewer than half of U.S. voters had even heard of the break-in. McGovern's attempt to make Watergate an election issue seemed the act of a desperate man.

After the election, rumors kept swirling and suspicious facts kept coming out. The wife of one of the burglars died in a plane crash while carrying ten thousand hundred-dollar bills. This money seemed to be hush money paid to one of the burglars to

By the time of this April 30, 1973 issue of Time *magazine, the Watergate scandal was national news.*

remain silent. Eventually, the Senate formed the Select Committee on Presidential Campaign Activities chaired by North Carolina senator Sam Ervin, who was determined to unravel the mystery of Watergate.

And it did unravel. One of the burglars, former CIA agent James McCord, admitted that he and others had been under pressure to stay silent. He named CRP chief John Mitchell as the man who had hired them. As the Senate's televised hearings went forward, Americans watched with rapt attention as they learned that White House involvement in the burglary went closer and closer to the top.

On April 30, 1973, Haldeman and Ehrlichman were forced to resign for their part in the cover-up. So was the president's lawyer, John Dean. Dean then testified that the president himself had authorized the payment of hush money to the burglars. Since Nixon denied any knowledge of the cover-up, it was simply Dean's word against the president's. The drama seemed to have reached a standstill—but not for long.

The Watergate Tapes

While testifying before the Ervin Committee, White House aide Alexander Butterfield was asked why a previous witness had suspected his conversation with the president was being tape-recorded. "I was hoping you fellows wouldn't ask me that," Butterfield replied. Then Butterfield revealed that Nixon had installed a voice-activated tape-recording system in his desk so he could keep a record of historic conversations. Nixon had intended the tapes to be for his own private use, but the Ervin Committee insisted that the tapes were evidence in a criminal case and demanded that Nixon release them. When Nixon refused to hand over the tapes, a constitutional crisis followed.

Just as Nixon's own credibility was coming under fire, his vice president was accused of having taken bribes while governor of Maryland. When these charges led to Agnew's resignation on October 10, 1973, Nixon appointed Michigan congressman Gerald Ford as the new vice president.

The scandalous resignation of the nation's second-highest official might have consumed the public attention for months, but it was almost completely overshadowed by the high drama of the Saturday Night Massacre. When Archibald Cox, a special prosecutor appointed to investigate Watergate, ordered Nixon to give him some of the tapes, Nixon offered to release only a summary of their contents. Cox refused the offer and repeated his demand that Nixon hand over the tapes.

Nixon was determined to keep the tapes to himself. On the evening of Saturday, October 20, Nixon ordered Cox's superior, Attorney General Elliot Richardson, to fire Cox. Richardson felt Cox had a right to demand the tapes, so Richardson refused to fire Cox and resigned himself. Then Nixon ordered Richardson's assistant, William D. Ruckelshaus, to fire Cox. He, too, refused and resigned. Only third-in-command Robert Bork was left to fire Cox. The events of this dramatic night made it appear that Nixon's own staff had lost respect for his authority.

Although Cox was finally gone, the pressure on Nixon only increased. Cox's replacement, Leon Jaworski, was just as insistent about getting the tapes as Cox had been. Nixon continued to offer compromises and deals, but no tapes. Finally, in a unanimous decision, the Supreme Court ruled that the president had to release the tapes.

Archibald Cox was chosen to be the special government prosecutor in the Watergate case.

Caught on Tape

Nixon had his Oval Office conversations taped so that he would have a record to use while writing his memoirs. He believed the tapes would support his version of history, while his enemies in the press and academics tried to tell it a different way. But the tapes did not support Nixon's public version of the Watergate crisis. They provided concrete evidence that he had been taking part in a cover-up of White House involvement in the crime.

Nixon claimed he did not know about the hush money paid to the burglars until March 1973. This conversation between the president and Haldeman in August 1972—only six weeks after the break-in—reveals that Nixon knew the Plumbers were being paid for their silence:

HALDEMAN: They've been taken care of. We've done a lot of discreet checking to be sure there's no discontent in the ranks, and there isn't any . . .

NIXON: At a considerable cost, I guess?

HALDEMAN: Yes.

NIXON: It's worth it.

HALDEMAN: It's very expensive. It's a costly . . .

NIXON: Well . . . they have to be paid. That's all there is to it.

In another taped conversation a few months later, when John Dean informed the president that the burglars wanted further payments of up to a million dollars, Nixon is heard saying the following:

NIXON: We could get that . . . you could get it in cash. I know where it could be gotten . . . no problem . . . . The money can be provided.

Besides bribing criminals for their silence, Nixon interfered with the justice system by encouraging White House employees to hide their knowledge of wrongdoing when called to testify in the Senate. In this conversation with John Mitchell, Nixon discusses the various ways to stonewall, or avoid cooperating in, the hearings:

(continued)

NIXON: I want you to stonewall it, let them plead the Fifth Amendment, cover-up or anything else, if it'll save it. . . . Just be damned sure you say "I don't remember; I can't recall. . . ."

Because Nixon knew what was on the tapes, he was determined to keep them to himself. When first asked to give the tapes to investigators, Nixon insisted that he could not because they contained information involving national security. Eventually, he offered to present a summary of the tapes with the national secrets left out. However, a comparison of Nixon's summaries with transcripts of the taped conversations shows that investigators were wise to refuse Nixon's offer. For example, Nixon summarized a conversation he had with John Dean like this:

NIXON: All John Mitchell is arguing then, is that now we use flexibility in order to get off the cover-up line.

The complete tapes reveal what Nixon actually said:

NIXON: All John Mitchell is arguing then, is that now we use flexibility in order to get on with the cover-up plan.

By changing *on with* to *off*, Nixon tried to make it seem that he was discouraging rather than supporting the cover-up. Such distinctions as this were enough to end the presidency of Richard Nixon.

When Nixon finally did hand over the tapes, it became clear why he had resisted for so long. In one conversation that took place on June 23, only six days after the burglars were arrested, Nixon can be heard ordering the FBI to stop looking into the break-in. This was the smoking gun—the clear, conclusive evidence prosecutors had been waiting for. It proved that Nixon knew about the break-in and attempted to cover it up. The president of the United States had overstepped the powers granted to him by the Constitution. He had broken the law.

Over the coming months, a close study of the tapes, along with testimonies from members of Nixon's administration, would reveal that the Watergate cover-up was only one of many legal and political transgressions for which Nixon was responsible. During his first term, Nixon had taken part in bugging, spying, lying, bribes, break-ins, and dirty tricks of every kind.

RESIGNATION

Hours after Nixon released the tapes to Congress, his few remaining supporters realized that the cause was lost. A group of prominent Republicans went to the White House to inform Nixon that he would be **impeached** and forced to leave office unless he resigned from the presidency, something no president had ever done.

On August 9, 1974, Nixon went on television to announce his resignation. "I am not a quitter," he said, "but America needs a full-time president. . . . Therefore, I shall resign the presidency effective at noon tomorrow." He never admitted actual wrongdoing in the Watergate affair, only mistakes of judgment.

When the TV cameras were gone, Nixon presented a more emotional speech to the White House staff. Near tears, he spoke of his father's struggles to make a living and his mother's suffering as her children died. He urged his friends not to be discouraged by failure or to become bitter by defeat. Then he crossed the White House lawn with Pat, stepped into the helicopter, and waved goodbye. As Gerald Ford was sworn in as the thirty-eighth president, Richard and Pat Nixon were in a plane halfway across the country, on their way back to California.

Richard Nixon boards the White House helicopter after resigning the presidency.

Elder Statesman Nixon

Upon his return to San Clemente, Nixon became extremely depressed. A senator who visited Nixon said he found him constantly on the verge of tears. Another visitor feared Nixon might even be suicidal. The former president did have cause for anxiety. Although his resignation had put an end to impeachment proceedings in Congress, it looked as though he would soon have to stand trial in criminal court for Watergate-related charges.

Almost as soon as Ford took office, he began to consider granting Nixon a **presidential pardon** to spare him the humiliation of going to court. With the former president in his weakened, depressed state, Ford wondered whether the stress of a drawn-out trial might actually kill him.

On September 8, 1974, Ford granted Nixon a pardon for any crimes he committed or might have committed while in the White House. In receiving the pardon Nixon did not admit guilt, but he did admit errors in judgment that left him feeling a "burden I shall bear for every day of life that is left for me." Nixon said that accepting the pardon was the greatest humiliation of his life.

Though Nixon would not be going to court, the legal help he had already needed left him with almost $2 million worth of bills to pay. He could not join a law firm to earn this money, because he had been disbarred from practicing law in California.

Hardly a week after the pardon, Nixon faced an even more immediate problem when he was forced to undergo surgery for a blood clot in his leg. After the surgery, internal bleeding caused his blood pressure to drop suddenly, and Nixon entered a state of shock. Nixon would later recall that as he lay near death for three hours, his mind and body hanging in the balance, he could see no reason to live. But he did live.

ANOTHER COMEBACK

As Haldeman, Ehrlichman, Dean, Mitchell, and others were sent to jail for Watergate-related crimes, Nixon recovered from his brush with death and began to pick up the pieces of his life. To pay off his debts, Nixon agreed to write his memoirs for an advance of

Nixon confers with his successors, presidents Jimmy Carter (left) and Gerald Ford.

$2.5 million. Slowly but surely, he became involved in political life again. In January 1975 Ford invited Nixon to provide advice about foreign affairs. Nixon submitted his words of wisdom under the code name Wizard. In 1976 the Chinese government extended Nixon an invitation for a return visit, and he eagerly accepted.

In 1977 Nixon faced the American people in a series of televised interviews with commentator David Frost. Nixon would never have subjected himself to these interviews except for the $600,000 payment, most of which went straight to his lawyers. Frost's questions were tough, but so was Nixon. He answered all questions frankly, without apologizing or backing down. About Watergate Nixon said, "I gave them the sword. And they stuck it in. And they twisted it with relish. And I guess if I'd been in their position I would have done the same thing."

Critics claimed Nixon was still trying to cover-up wrongdoing, but many Americans were impressed by the former president's frankness. By 1978 Nixon's reputation was clearly on the upswing. A poll ranked him one of the ten most admired men in the world.

In 1980 Richard and Pat Nixon moved to a penthouse in New York City. There Nixon threw high-profile parties for his powerful Republican friends, some of whom were now serving the new president, Ronald Reagan. He kept as busy as ever by writing books about foreign policy and accepting frequent speaking engagements. He also began appearing at official ceremonies,

Nixon speaks at the dedication of the Richard Nixon Presidential Library.

such as the funeral of Egyptian president Anwar Sadat, where he sat alongside former presidents Carter and Ford.

In July 1990 Nixon was honored by the presence of Ford, Carter, Reagan, and George H. W. Bush at the opening of the Nixon Presidential Library in Yorba Linda, California. By then Republicans were honoring Nixon publicly and openly praising his achievements, and leaders of both parties were seeking his advice. After the humiliation of Watergate, his reputation had been nearly restored.

It was during the term of the next president, Democrat Bill Clinton, that the end came for both Richard and Pat Nixon. When Pat died of lung cancer in 1993, her husband of fifty-three years wept openly at the funeral. On April 22, 1994, Nixon himself had a stroke and died at the age of eighty-one.

President Bill Clinton at the funeral of Richard Nixon, April 27, 1994.

At a memorial service following Nixon's death, Clinton and four former presidents went with their families to Yorba Linda to pay their respects. It was the largest gathering of presidential families ever assembled. After a series of distinguished political figures praised Nixon as "an elder statesman" and "a hero," President Clinton summed up Nixon's achievements. Clinton was the only speaker to allude, even slightly, to the crisis that had marred Nixon's presidency, when he said, "May the day of judging President Nixon on anything less than his entire life and career come to a close."

Today, historians are beginning to do just what Clinton suggested: to try to see Watergate as merely one part of the long and varied career of Richard Nixon. In particular, many historians are coming to revise their view of Nixon's domestic achievements. Since the Reagan presidency, American government has become more conservative. Although in the 1970s liberals tended to criticize Nixon's domestic policies, today many liberals appreciate his achievements in civil rights, social welfare, the environment, and the arts. Members of both parties praise him for establishing such programs as the Environmental Protection Agency, which endure to this day.

Nixon's handling of the Vietnam War, however, is not so highly praised as it was when he claimed to have brought peace with honor. As Watergate dragged on, the North Vietnamese broke the peace agreement and moved into the South, which eventually fell in 1975. Of the 58,000 American lives lost during the Vietnam War, almost 21,000 were lost during Nixon's presidency, as were the lives of hundreds of thousands of Vietnamese.

Nixon's glorious trip to China is still praised today. And his easing of the strain with the Soviets is seen as a first step that

The Characters of Nixon

As historians debate the true nature of Nixon's character, artists working on stage and screen have concocted an extraordinary variety of Nixons. Oliver Stone's movie *Nixon* (1995) presents Nixon as a dark, stiff, bitter man with a drinking problem. Andrew Fleming's movie *Dick* (1999) presents Nixon as a jovial, but short-tempered father figure who proves to be bumbling and foolish. David Edgar's play *Dick Deterred* (1974) models Nixon on England's villainous King Richard the Third, a cunning, evil tyrant. Russell Lees's play *Nixon's Nixon* (1995) depicts Nixon as a gabby, theatrical, and extremely sensitive man with a wild imagination.

Perhaps the most flattering Nixon character appears in John Adams and Alice Goodman's opera *Nixon in China* (1987). This musical extravaganza presents a Nixon who is fascinated and deeply affected by the historic events unfolding around him. In the opera's most powerful moment, when Nixon steps from his plane to greet Chou En-Lai, the music and striking visual imagery capture the bizarre thrill of contact being made between two utterly separate worlds. It is a gripping depiction of a great moment in American history that surely would have moved the real Nixon.

eventually helped lead to the end of the Soviet Union and the fall of communism in Eastern Europe.

However, none of Nixon's achievements dim the memory of Watergate, which has proven to be one of the most influential events in American history. In the wake of Watergate, a series of laws were passed to control campaign practices and to limit presidential power. But the main change was a shift in the way

Americans regard politicians. Before Watergate, Americans might suspect their presidents of being flawed. Since Watergate, however, presidents are commonly suspected of being liars and crooks. This attitude is reflected by members of the press, who feel justified in looking into the personal lives of any and all political figures. Politicians, in turn, are "handled" and packaged more carefully than ever so that they might survive this extreme scrutiny.

While examining his achievements, historians continue to ask who Nixon really was and to ponder why he did what he did. Millions of documents relating to his administration are now available. Yet, not one of them explains why Nixon was so committed to bending and breaking the rules in his fight to win an election that he had no real chance of losing. Or why Nixon saw anyone who ran against him as an enemy who had to be destroyed. How could anyone combine the shrewdness Nixon showed in winning the presidency with the foolishness he displayed in losing it.

In trying to come to grips with the character of Nixon, former Nixon administration official Dean Burch reaches a grim conclusion. "The man didn't believe in anything," Burch claims. "He didn't believe in religion or principle or anything." Similarly, Gary Wills claims Nixon was so devoted to creating an image of himself that it is impossible to know who he really was.

Joan Hoff, a historian who interviewed Nixon several times in person, feels otherwise. Hoff argues that Nixon was in fact more genuine and more deeply committed to certain principles than many presidents who have come since. Looking back, it is certainly clear where Nixon stood on major issues. In foreign affairs he was a hawk, deeply opposed to the spread of communism, who ended up working with Communists for the sake of peace. In terms of domestic issues, he was a moderate, anxious to appease Conservatives while supporting social-welfare programs that helped others help themselves.

While Nixon's belief in certain ideals was consistent throughout his career, so were certain character flaws. He saw politics as a nasty game in which one had to be vicious and dishonest to win. His vengeful spirit and his willingness to break rules led to his downfall, and to the image many people have of Nixon as crafty and dishonest.

But if one follows Clinton's advice and takes in the whole picture, there is another quality with which Nixon's name might be associated: persistence. Every time Nixon fell, no matter how hard he got hit, he always got back up and returned to the fight.

On Nixon's historic visit to China, Chou En-Lai praised Nixon's ability to come back from defeat, saying "men who travel on a smooth road all their lives do not develop strength." Nixon echoed this idea in his last speech as president, when he told his staff, "Only if you have been in the deepest valley can you ever know how magnificent it is to be on the highest mountain." Whatever one may think of Nixon, there is no denying that he journeyed to the deepest valley of American public life—and to the highest mountain.

Over the course of his turbulent career, Nixon experienced crushing defeats and glorious triumphs.

TIMELINE

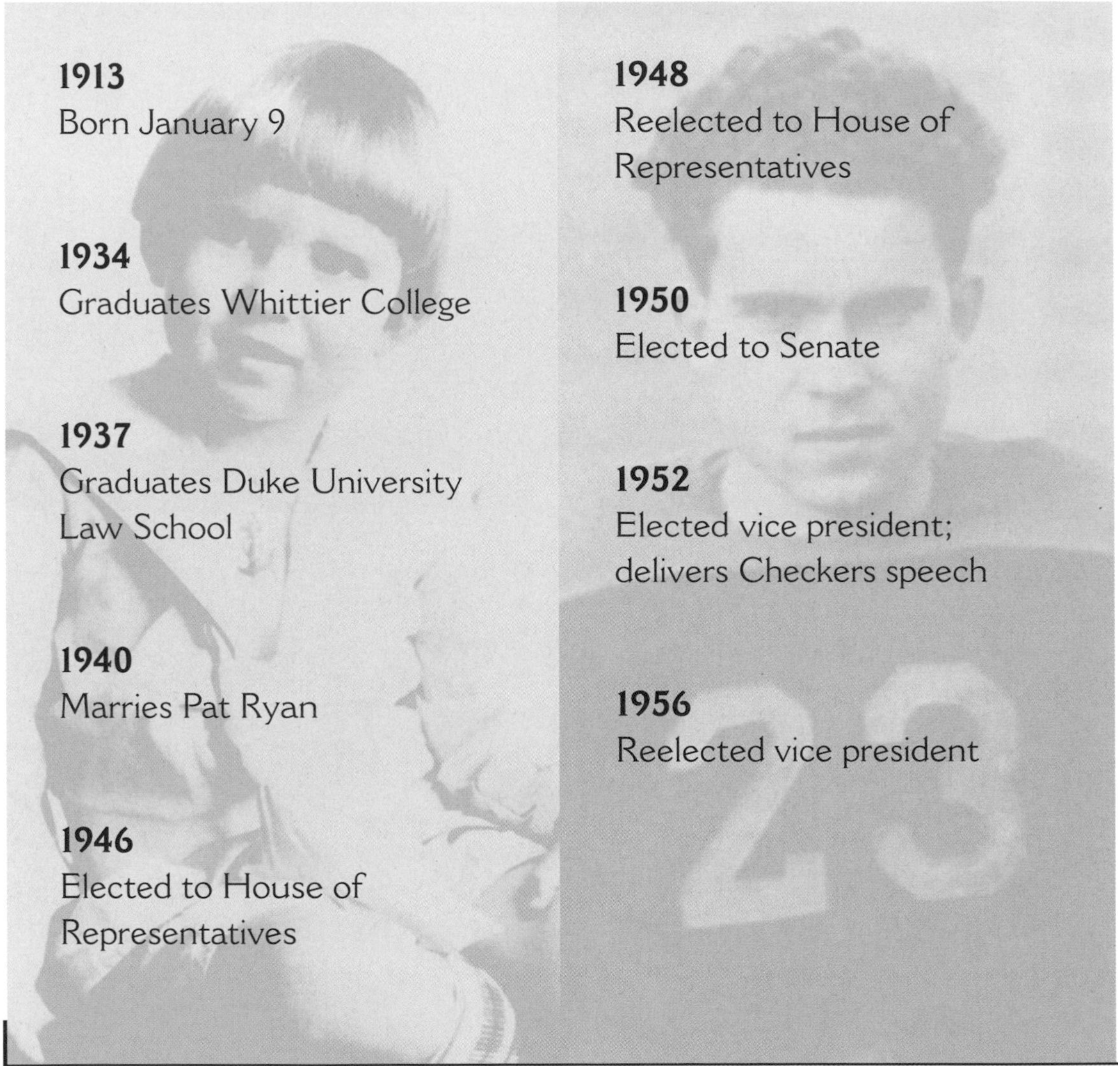

1913
Born January 9

1934
Graduates Whittier College

1937
Graduates Duke University
Law School

1940
Marries Pat Ryan

1946
Elected to House of
Representatives

1948
Reelected to House of
Representatives

1950
Elected to Senate

1952
Elected vice president;
delivers Checkers speech

1956
Reelected vice president

1910

1959
Visits soviet leader Nikita Khrushchev

1960
Defeated for president

1962
Defeated for governor

1968
Elected president

1971
Visits Communist China premier Chou En-Lai

1972
Reelected president; the Plumbers break into Democratic headquarters at the Watergate Hotel

1974
Resigns the presidency; pardoned by President Gerald Ford

1994
Dies April 22

2000

GLOSSARY

containment the policy of stopping the spread of an enemy's territory or power

détente a relaxing of tension between rivals

dove a person who advocated ending the Vietnam War

hawk a person who supported the Vietnam War

impeached to be removed from office, especially for improper conduct

liberals those who favor new ideas, tending to support change

moderate favoring a middle ground between liberal and conservative policies

moratorium a suspension of planned activity

negative income tax money paid by the government to people of low income

presidential pardon an official act in which the president grants forgiveness and protection from punishment for a particular misdeed

revenue sharing the passing of funds from the federal government to officials in state and local governments who in turn see that the funds are distributed to those in need

slush fund a fund raised for various unspecified purposes

Vietnamization during the Vietnam War, the process of turning over the responsibility for defending South Vietnam to the South Vietnamese, thereby allowing American forces to withdraw

FURTHER INFORMATION

BOOKS

Anderson, Dale. *Watergate: Scandal in the White House* (Snapshots in History). Mankato, MN: Compass Point Books, 2006.

Barron, Rachel Stiffler. *Richard Nixon: American Politician* (Notable Americans). Greensboro, NC: Morgan Reynolds Publishing, 2004.

Ochester, Betsy. *Richard M. Nixon: America's 37th President* (Encyclopedia of Presidents, Second Series). Danbury, CT: Children's Press, 2005.

WEB SITES

The American President: Richard Nixon

www.americanpresident.org/history/richardnixon

This site grants access to Nixon's public papers and White House tapes and provides a detailed biography based on the PBS series and a multimedia presentation.

The Richard Nixon Library and Birthplace

www.nixonfoundation.org

Visit this site for a tour of the most active presidential museum in the United States, the Richard Nixon Museum.

BIBLIOGRAPHY

Hoff, Joan. *Nixon Reconsidered*. New York: BasicBooks, 1994.

Manchester, William. *The Glory and the Dream*. New York: Bantam Books, 1974.

Nixon, Richard. *In the Arena*. New York: Simon and Schuster, 1990.

———. *The Memoirs of Richard Nixon*. New York: Simon and Schuster, 1978.

Small, Melvin. *The Presidency of Richard Nixon*. Lawrence, KS: University of Kansas Press, 1999.

Strober, Deborah Hart and Gerald S. *Nixon: An Oral History of His Presidency*. New York: HarperCollins, 1990.

Summers, Anthony. *The Arrogance of Power: The Secret World of Richard Nixon*. New York: Viking Press, 2000.

Wead, Doug. *All the President's Children*. New York: Atria Books, 2003.

INDEX

Pages in **boldface** are illustrations.

ABOUT THE AUTHOR

Billy Aronson's plays have been produced by Playwrights Horizons, Ensemble Studio Theatre, Wellfleet Harbor Actors Theater, and Woolly Mammoth Theatre; published in *Best American Short Plays*; and awarded a New York Foundation for the Arts grant. His writing for the musical theater includes the original concept and additional lyrics for the Broadway musical *Rent*. His TV writing includes scripts for the Cartoon Network's *Courage, the Cowardly Dog*, MTV's *Beavis & Butt-Head*, Nickelodeon's *Wonder Pets* (head writer), Noggin's *Upside Down Show*, PBS's *Carmen Sandiego*, and *Postcards from Buster*, for which he received an Emmy nomination. He also wrote *Ulysses S. Grant* for Marshall Cavendish's Presidents and Their Times series. Aronson lives in Brooklyn with his wife, Lisa Vogel, and their children, Jake and Anna. For a good time visit www.billyaronson.com.

748-2855